PRAY
this...

Prayer Nuggets from the Bible
for the Modern Christian Woman

Emmanuella
Ofurie

For more information, email nuellasnuggets@gmail.com

ISBN: 979-8-89109-031-6 - paperback

ISBN: 979-8-89109-034-7 - ebook

Did you know?
You're a nugget!

You read that right! Allow me to explain.

In 2018, I didn't have a word for how I felt. I had no self-love or confidence and felt depressed, but I had GOD.

One day, the Holy Spirit whispered, "You're a nugget."

I laughed. "Like a chicken nugget?"

He said no, which was good because I prefer a burger.

"Like the Denver Nuggets Basketball Team?" I tried again. He said no, which was also good because I'm not a sports fan.

He then asked me to search it. When I took to Google, I got this:

a small lump of gold or other precious metal found ready-formed in the earth

With time, I realized he was right—about all of us. Each of us has a combination of gifts God gave us that makes us unique, and we often need little reminders of this, little golden nuggets of our own. This is why I created the Nuella's Nuggets community!

Check out my YouTube video titled WELCOME!!! | Nuellas' Nuggets Vision & Mission | Join the #NUGGETS FAM for a detailed explanation of what it means to be a nugget. Subscribe for lifestyle videos from a faith-based perspective!

DEDICATION

This book is dedicated to my family, my friends and the churches that have nourished me with God's Word and provided me with a community of believers.

TABLE OF CONTENTS

Prayers for You

Prayers for Others and Things Bigger Than Yourself

LETTER TO THE READER

Dear Reader,

Have you ever wondered <u>exactly</u> what Jesus wants us to pray for?

As the pastor's kid, I quickly developed a solid prayer life. I grew up in Nigeria, West Africa, where the church culture is very different from that of the churches on the North Shore of Massachusetts where I now reside. In Nigeria, most of our prayers were for binding devils and casting demons. My prayer vocabulary included "die," "back to the sender," and "catch fire"—and those prayers worked. However, my urge to explore another part of prayer took me on a journey to write this book, *Pray this*.

I started to pen chapters of this book one day while I was at work. I had just finished listening to Christine Caine's *The Best Work* video series in which she mentioned Matthew 9:38:

"The harvest is plentiful, but the laborers are few; therefore pray earnestly to the Lord of the harvest to send out laborers into his harvest."[1]

I had heard this scripture many times, but this time it hit me differently. I heard it in such a way that it unlocked a desire to know what else Jesus asked us to pray for.

As a woman of faith, it can be tricky to navigate what advice to listen to. I say listen directly to God. He has exact

---

1   English Standard Version (ESV)

instructions for women as to how to pray, what to pray for, and even when to pray so that your prayers may be answered and you may affect the most people and lead souls to Him. This book is filled with those bits of gold that God left for women to find within the pages of His book. He has a special plan for us, ladies. Let's follow the trail in wisdom and see.

If you have been praying and wondering why your prayers go unanswered, read this book. It is a treasure trove of the **exact** prayers God asked us all to pray through the voices of both men and women. Your prayer life will take a new turn as you dive into this book. It will change your posture from only thinking about your needs to wanting God's entire will to be done on earth as it is in heaven.

Not all prayers that go unanswered are selfish prayers, but God is more likely to answer a prayer for Him to use us to enlarge His kingdom than one that asks for a higher paying job, a fancy car, or any material thing that may cause one to lose their soul. For what will it profit a man to gain the whole world but lose his soul? One can argue we need these material possessions, but many are quick to forget their promises and vows when they get their material blessings. The goal is to be part of the answer to other people's prayers. The goal is not just for God to do small favors for you that will only sustain you in the short term. There needs to be a constant flow of love among <u>all</u> of His children as much as possible—and God told us exactly how to accomplish this with the Word.

Prayer is for building a relationship with our Heavenly Father. When we pray for others, we benefit from those prayers. When you pray for someone who has hurt you, you release that person from your heart—and you receive the blessing of freedom and peace! You no longer carry that baggage of hurt, resentment, and anger.

Blessings are not always tangible. We need to develop the skills to identify the spiritual benefits of joy, peace, love, patience, gentleness, and faithfulness, all of which are granted to us by the Holy Spirit and help us pray and take action.

This book is for the believer who wants to stop praying selfish prayers and start praying for our brothers and sisters in Christ who are in sin, for the lost souls, for our pastors and leaders, for those who hurt us and persecute us, and for more people to say yes to kingdom work. You will begin to see your prayers answered like never before as you PRAY *this*.

Don't wait! Pray the prayer and watch God show up!

INTRODUCTION

"What causes fights and quarrels among you? Don't they come from your desires that battle within you? You desire but do not have, so you kill. You covet but you cannot get what you want, so you quarrel and fight. You do not have because you do not ask God. When you ask, you do not receive, because you ask with wrong motives, that you may spend what you get on your pleasures."
James 4:1-3 (NIV)

I don't know about you, but this excerpt from the book of James makes me feel called out—particularly the part about "wrong motives." This is most of us, which is why you see so many people feeling so unfulfilled in their lives. So, what is the right way to pray? I can tell you right now that it's not to pray harder or more consistently. It's actually to take the focus off of you—and to do *this* consistently!

Intercessory prayer is where you pray for somebody else's needs. You can pray for your friends, your family, your church, your country, or pretty much anyone or anything the Holy Spirit lays on your heart. It truly is the way to connect to something bigger than yourself, and thus God rewards it with speed!

Of course, we are all human and we have our needs and wants, so there are specific things the Bible has told us we can pray for ourselves (which we will go over in Part 1), but once our bases are covered so that our own belief is strong, we must let that prayer naturally lead to asking God to help those around us, including institutions, large groups of people, entire countries, and even the world. Intercessory prayer can be done by yourself, it can be done with your spouse, or even with an entire group of believers at church prayer meetings.

God ultimately wishes for us to be intercessors, especially as women. We contain special gifts that have not always been celebrated, but I do believe today's woman is the perfect candidate to carry out true and selfless intercessory prayer. As women, we are leaders of our families and congregations in very unique ways. We see and feel what others sometimes don't, therefore making us more sensitive to the needs of others.

One of the most important aspects of a Christian's life in general is intercessory prayer. It really is what makes the world go 'round. It is a powerful way to pray, and the best part is that it is available to everyone. Part 2 is all about acquiring this valuable skill to enrich your prayer practice—and your life as a whole!

Each chapter contains a song to listen to while reflecting on the scriptures presented, along with some journal prompts and blank pages to write your reflections on. Feel free to jot down any additional notes that speak to you on your Bible study journey.

God wants you to have your needs, but He wants you to consider others, and this is where intercessory prayer feeds your own life because you create favor in the Lord's eyes, being someone who takes care of His children. Intercessory prayer is where we are so concerned for someone else that it moves us to pray for them. God does not take this lightly. It's such a wonderful thing for Christians to come together and cry out to God for those around them. May God compel you to engage in the art of intercessory prayer.

PART 1

PRAYERS FOR YOU

"She considers a field and buys it; out of her earnings she plants a vineyard. She sets about her work vigorously; her arms are strong for her tasks."
—Proverbs 31:16-17 (NIV)

Let's begin by focusing on you. You probably pray for yourself every day—I know I do! And why wouldn't you, right? As much as it is important to pray for others and the world, it is also God's will that you pray for strength for yourself. How else would you be able to do God's work? It is crucial to "pour from a full cup," as they say, and it all starts with nourishing the existent relationship you have with God, no matter where you are along your journey.

When it comes to prayer, it is important first and foremost to know deep in your soul that God loves you and wants the best for you—yes you! The individual that you are. You are a gift perfectly crafted by God himself, so take care of yourself so you can take care of others.

I cherish my regular prayer routine and have felt God so present in my heart that I wish to share this experience with you

WISDOM

> She speaks with wisdom,
> and faithful instruction is on her tongue."
> -Proverbs 31:26 (NIV)

Along my prayer path, I have found that God is more than happy to help with matters of the mind. He is there first and foremost to make sure we are at peace mentally so we may have a sober enough mind to discern the actions He wants us to take. We must be at peace to speak the truth He wants us to speak—and to hear the truth He wants us to hear.

We need the wisdom of God to think, do and act right, and all we have to do is ASK. James says: "If any of you lacks wisdom, let him ask God, who gives generously to all without reproach, and it will be given him." (James 1:5-8 [ESV])

Interestingly enough, these days it is so easy to access knowledge, but many people are devoid of wisdom. What stands between knowledge and wisdom?

I'll tell you right now: it comes down to human nature. It's pride.

Pride Blocks Blessings

We are know-it-alls. We pride ourselves on knowing the answers, flaunt our knowledge, and are basically always seeking our opportunity to speak!

I love to pick out the silent people in a crowd. One might think they're the ones who are clueless, but often they are the most thoughtful individuals, patient enough to take the time to construct a meaningful response rather than jumping to say the first thing that comes to mind.

If you're anything like me, you say the first thing on your mind. You probably classify yourself as straightforward. You don't beat around the bush. You tell the truth, even if it's a bit harsh. As Christians, we of course concern ourselves with the truth, but God also wants us to read the room—and check our pride.

Humility is the opposite of pride. It is a trait God wants us to have, especially in prayer. In Luke 18:9-14 (AMP), Jesus tells a parable that was addressed to people who:

1. Trusted in themselves above God
2. Were confident that they were righteous (posing outwardly as upright and in right standing with God)
3. Viewed others with contempt

Jesus compared a Pharisee and a tax collector who went to the temple to pray:

> "The Pharisee stood [ostentatiously] and began praying to himself [in a self-righteous way, saying]: 'God, I thank You that I am not like the rest of men—swindlers, unjust (dishonest), adulterers—or even like this tax collector. I fast twice a week; I pay tithes of all that I get.' But the tax collector, standing at a distance, would not even raise his eyes toward heaven, but was striking his chest [in humility and repentance], saying, 'God, be merciful and gracious to me, the [especially wicked] sinner [that I am]!'"

Our posture in prayer should reflect that of the tax collector, not thinking we are better than others but rather dealing with each other in love and humility.

This reminds me of Abigail and her wisdom in handling the issue with her husband and David.[2] Samuel, David's mentor,

---

had died and was buried, and afterwards, David, distraught, went to the wilderness of Paran.

Abigail, the wife of Nabal (a very wealthy man with many sheeps and goats), was an "intelligent and beautiful woman, but her husband was surly and mean in his dealings," which soon proved to be a problem.

It was sheep shearing time, which was a time of lavish hospitality towards others, and it was historically commemorated as a feast with enough food for everyone, so David sent 10 young men to Nabal to receive any gifts Nabal would give. David had been good to Nabal by guarding his flocks when Philistine raids were common. And David waited for the appropriate time to request payment when Nabal received a large harvest.

Nabal acted like he did not know David and belittled him by claiming he was a disobedient servant to Saul. Nabal was stingy and uncaring, repaying David with evil for his good.

David took action as a strong fighter and warrior and took approximately 400 armed men to Nabal's home. When Abigail heard of this, she hurried and took bread, wine, sheep, raisins, and fig cakes and rode on a donkey towards David and his men.

When Abigail saw David, she quickly dismantled from the donkey and got on her knees in respect. She took the blame for her husband, asked for forgiveness, and sang praises of David thus restoring his dignity and preventing bloodshed for her household.

Wisdom Is Just a Prayer Away

So, where do we start? How can we get this wisdom the Book of Proverbs talks about? Proverbs 9:10 says, "The fear of the Lord is the beginning of wisdom."[3] The fear of the Lord here speaks to having reverence for God. It speaks of being humble enough to say, "I don't know it all, and I need your wisdom." Proverbs 31:30 says, "Charm is deceptive, and beauty is fleeting, but a woman who fears the Lord is to be praised."[4]

Wisdom is available to you. We all need wisdom for different things. You may need wisdom when you're single, in your career, throughout your marriage, when bringing up your children in the Lord, to be a woman of integrity in your workplace—and you can have it by humbly asking.

When I'm feeling weak, I find little pockets of time throughout the day to spend time with God. I cry out, "Lord, please be my strength." I do it even when I'm working on a difficult homework problem. I say, "Lord, help me. You said, 'The memory of the righteous is blessed,'[5] so bless my mind to solve this question." When I'm anxious, I pray for the peace of God and sing "Tremble" by Mosaic MSC or "God I Look to You" by Bethel Music.

---

3   English Standard Version (ESV)
4   New International Version (NIV)
5   Proverbs 10:17 (NKJV)

So, let us PRAY *this*:

Heavenly Father, you said in James 1:5 that if anyone lacks wisdom, let him ask for it. Today, I humble myself before you. Sometimes I think, say, and do things that I shouldn't. I want to be more careful of what I allow into my heart. Please give me the grace to listen to the nudging of the Holy Spirit and to obey. Please give me the wisdom to act according to your Word and desires. In Jesus's Name. Amen.

Reflection

Listen to the song "God I Look to You" by Bethel Music and use the following prompts to kick off your reflection on this chapter, which you can write in the blank pages provided.

1. Where could you benefit from God's wisdom in your life?

2. Is it difficult to take the posture of humility in your dealings with people? Why?

WORRY AND ANXIETY

"Do not be anxious about anything, but in every situation, by prayer and petition, with thanksgiving, present your requests to God."
-Philippians 4:6 (NIV)

I'm certain you were worrying about something in the past 24 hours. I'm talking about things we as humans often worry about that take up more space than they should. The worst part about these worries is that we can't control the outcome, yet we still go on and on in our heads trying to find ways to change our circumstances.

Unfortunately, worry is such a part of our daily life that it becomes something we're accustomed to. The act of worrying leads to anxiety, which plagues 60 percent of U.S. adults. As valid as our worries may be, they lead to anxiety, and the cure for anxiety is, ironically, to STOP WORRYING.

What a mess! Let's unpack this funny little phenomenon for a second.

I recently applied for a job that would double my income, and since I submitted that application, I did not stop worrying. I kept thinking to myself, "I know I am qualified for the position...I had a cover letter and submitted the application in the first 14 days...The start date for the job is July 2023, and I submitted the application in March...but if I continue to worry, I'll be worrying for months..."

Where did these thoughts get me? Nowhere. Worrying is the opposite of trusting God.

On top of feeding anxiety, depression, and issues with memory and focus, worrying has been shown to contribute to physical ailments, such as:

- headaches
- sleep issues
- digestive problems
- weight gain or loss
- muscle pain
- stroke
- high blood pressure
- heart disease

If this isn't enough incentive to stop worrying, I don't know what is. And if you've already experienced any of these symptoms, you need to ask God for help in stopping these negative mental patterns from arising. They are only making things worse.

There's a lyric in the song "I'll Give Thanks" by Housefires that I love so much. It says: "Why do I worry? God knows what I need."

Jesus speaking to us in Matthew 6:26 (AMP) invites us to "look at the birds of the air; they neither sow [seed] nor reap [the harvest] nor gather [the crops] into barns, and yet your heavenly Father keeps feeding them. Are you not worth much more than they are?"

And if we are worried about clothes, He invites us to "see how the lilies and wildflowers of the field grow; they do not labor nor do they spin [wool to make clothing], yet I say to you that not even Solomon in all his glory and splendor dressed himself like one of these. But if God so clothes the grass of the field, which is alive and green today and tomorrow is [cut and] thrown [as fuel] into the furnace, will He not much more clothe you? You of little faith!"[6]

Although our worries may be greater than "What are we going to eat?" or "What are we going to drink?" or "What are we going to wear?", Jesus tells us not to worry or be anxious, "for your heavenly Father knows that you need them."[7] In fact, when you find yourself wanting more than your basic needs, it is a good opportunity to stop and be grateful that you even have the basic necessities of food, water, and clothes that a lot of people do not have. Had you not these things, you would not be in a position to ask for more.

---

6   Matthew 6:28-30 (AMP)
7   Matthew 6:32 (AMP)

Think back to the times God answered your call, whether it was for basic necessities or for something beyond. Collect evidence so that when your faith begins to waver, your focus always comes back to God. After your answers in the Reflection section provided at the end of this chapter, make a note of every time God answered your prayers. Refer to this list as many times as needed, maybe even adding the specific scriptures you were pondering at the moment.

No matter how far we stray, God always welcomes our efforts to reconnect with Him.

The Cure for Anxiety

One day, my youngest brother Jesse was at school and he wasn't feeling well, so he visited the nurse's office. The nurse's diagnosis was STRESS!!! A 16-year-old high school student was so stressed he couldn't focus on his studies. It turned out that the origin of his stress was the lack of offers from colleges to play football. In comparison to his older brother Sam, who had received many offers by the time he was a junior, Jesse had not received a single one. The fear of the unknown and the future had weighed heavily on him.

I tried my best to help him relieve his stress. I filled the room with eucalyptus candles, rubbed his temples with cream that had eucalyptus in it, and placed drops of eucalyptus essential oil on his bed.

Okay, I went hard on the eucalyptus—but I also played him Christian meditation songs before he slept. We continued this practice for a few more days before his game at the end of the week. All of my efforts helped, but I knew I could not keep up with all of that.

So, I armored him with one last thing: the Word of God. I made sure he memorized Philippians 4:6-7 (NIV): "Do not be anxious about anything, but in every situation, by prayer and petition, with thanksgiving, present your requests to God. And the peace of God, which transcends all understanding, will guard your hearts and your minds in Christ Jesus."

It was fun seeing him repeat this verse. I would catch him off guard as we would go about our day and ask, "What's our scripture?" He'd think about it a little, try to quote it, and sometimes reach for the Bible app to crosscheck if he got it. That was the best gift I could have given him for that situation. It calmed his worry and switched our focus to God.

Offers from Havard, Duke, and Princeton are only a fraction of what Jesse got. He is now committed to playing Division 1 football at Rutgers University. If you ask me, I don't even know why he was worrying in the first place. God knows all of what we'll ever need.

So, when you pray, don't worry or be anxious about anything. Make your requests known to God and allow His peace that passes all understanding to guide you in Jesus.

Notice the scripture didn't say, "God will answer all requests." God's answer for your worry and anxiety is peace. If your request goes against peace, He may not grant it. God wants to keep you in perfect peace first and foremost.

So, let us PRAY *this*:

Heavenly Father, I get into the habit of worrying about everything, and I'm so anxious about my future. Please help me to stop worrying and trust that you will tend to all my needs according to your riches and glory. May your peace that passeth all understanding fill me. In Jesus's Name. Amen.

Reflection

Listen to the song "I'll Give Thanks" by Housefires and use the following prompts to kick off your reflection on this chapter, which you can write in the blank pages provided.

1. What are you currently worrying about?
2. How has God answered your prayers in the past?

FASTING

Nowadays, people fast from social media, which is great! In fact, I've tried to fast from television. God knows we need it, with the bad news, derogatory music, and sexualized images we're exposed to daily. While abstaining from those activities can be considered a fast, biblical fasting takes it to the next level: you're putting aside food for a while to focus solely on God. People typically engage in 12-hour, 14-hour, 16-hour or full-day fasts.

Growing up as the pastor's kid, fasting was a normal occurrence. I remember my dad encouraging us to wait one more hour until after prayer to break our fast at 1 pm.

That extra hour felt like forever. I had no energy to hold on and my stomach made loud noises alerting others of my hungry predicament! As I've grown older, however, I have held personal fasts to get closer to God, in expectation of things like a job after school. Fasting is a beautiful depiction of our trust in God. When we fast, we are relying on His Word to be bread for our soul. It is the living water to quench our thirst. It elevates our prayer and strengthens our belief.

Fasting gives us the authority to cast out unclean spirits: Jesus replied to His disciples when they inquired why they couldn't cast out the demon from a boy but Jesus could. Jesus said: "This kind [of unclean spirit] cannot come out by anything but prayer and fasting [to the Father]." (Mark 9:29 [AMP])

Fasting gives space to the Holy Spirit to speak to us: "While they [Christians] were serving the Lord and fasting, the Holy Spirit said, 'Set apart for Me Barnabas and Saul [Paul] for the work to which I have called them.' Then after fasting and praying, they laid their hands on them [in approval and dedication] and sent them away [on their first journey]" (Acts 13:3 [AMP]).

Remember how I said this section is all about you? Well, that includes your health. God wants you to be in optimal physical condition so you may carry out the life path He carved for you. The Bible encourages fasting because not only are the spiritual benefits vast—the health benefits of fasting are seemingly endless. Fasting:

- lowers blood sugar and blood pressure
- enhances digestive, brain, and heart health
- supports faster recovery from injuries

- decreases inflammation and signs of aging
- aids the recycling of cells and promotes longevity
- improves body composition, encourages fat loss, and helps build muscle

While there are many physical benefits to fasting, the purpose of fasting in this book is spiritual. Fasting is not to prove to people that you can go without food or water for a long period of time. Fasting develops fruits of the Spirit in us that make us mature Christians. Fasting is oil in the lamp. Fasting sets us apart and increases our spiritual antenna to listen to the voice of God. Most importantly, fasting is a weapon. It prepares us to approach situations differently.

In order for it to be effective when we fast, we need to be mindful of where our heart is while we're doing it. In Isaiah 58, the Israelites set up a fast, but it was not pleasing unto God. When we fast, we are to heed the message of Jesus:

"Do not look somber as the hypocrites do, for they disfigure their faces to show others they are fasting. Truly I tell you, they have received their reward in full. But when you fast, put oil on your head and wash your face, so that it will not be obvious to others that you are fasting, but only to your Father, who is unseen; and your Father, who sees what is done in secret, will reward you."
—Matthew 6:16-18 (NIV)

As we talk about fasting, I am reminded of Esther, whose people were condemned to death by her husband, King Xerxes. When Mordecai, Esther's uncle, relayed the terrible news to her through her eunuchs and female attendants, "she was in great distress." Esther had only two choices in this matter: to approach the king or to wait until she was summoned to place her request. In this era, no man or woman could approach the king in the inner court without being summoned by the king himself.

As expected, Esther was scared to approach the king, and thirty days had passed since she was last summoned by the king, but she approached him anyway. When Mordecai received Esther's words, he replied: "Do not think that because you are in the king's house you alone of all the Jews will escape. For if you remain silent at this time, relief and deliverance for the Jews will arise from another place, but you and your father's family will perish." (Esther 4:12-14 [NIV])

Upon hearing this, Esther sent word back, saying: "Go, gather together all the Jews who are in Susa, and fast for me. Do not eat or drink for three days, night or day. I and my attendants will fast as you do. When this is done, I will go to the king, even though it is against the law. And if I perish, I perish." (Esther 4:15-16 [NIV])

The penalty for anyone, including Queen Esther who entered the king's inner court without being summoned, was death, but the king ended up extending his gold scepter and sparing her life. The fast served as an armor for Esther and brought

God's favor as she approached the king. Fasting gave her courage, even though there was a fifty percent chance she would be killed. Fasting gave Esther wisdom on how to handle the matter of the Jews being wiped out in all the provinces when the man who initiated this genocide was elevated by her husband, King Xerxus, higher than all the other nobles. Fasting will give you power, courage, and wisdom.

So, let us PRAY *this*:

Heavenly Father, I understand the benefit of fasting and want to experience it in my life. However, I can barely carve out the time. Life is busy and every time I decide to fast, something happens that changes the agenda. Please help me make fasting a regular spiritual discipline. I receive the grace to pause physical food as I replenish my Spirit with your Word, prayer, and songs while dwelling in your presence. In Jesus's Name. Amen.

Resource: "Fasting" by Jentenzen Franklin.

Reflection

Listen to the song "Wait On You" by Elevation Worship and Maverick City Music and use the following prompts to kick off your reflection on this chapter, which you can write in the blank pages provided.

1. What do you need to fast from—and for—today?

2. How can you make fasting a consistent spiritual discipline?

TEMPTATIONS

I fell into countless temptations as a young Christian and wondered why God would allow this to happen. The truth is: temptation is an unavoidable part of our Christian walk. In fact, it is necessary for spiritual growth and development. But we often miss the difference between God's testing and the devil's temptations. God does not tempt us to sin, but He does test us.

Bible.org has an etymological perspective that will help you decipher temptations from tests and interpret events that happen to you in the most conducive way to your Christian path:

"The same Greek term is used in the New Testament for testing and tempting. What distinguishes temptation from testing is the intended outcome. Satan tempts us, with the intended (or at least hoped for) outcome of our failure. God tests us, with the intended outcome of our proven faithfulness. However, the same event can be both a temptation and a test just like how God allowed Satan to afflict Job (Job 1 & 2)."[8]

In Matthew 26, Jesus went to Gethsemane to pray, and His disciples followed Him. In the gospel of Luke, it is recorded that before He left His disciples to go further to pray, He said: "Pray that you will not fall into temptation." (Luke 22:40 [NIV])

But when He came back, He found them asleep and said unto Peter: "Watch and pray so that you will not fall into temptation. The Spirit is willing, but the flesh is weak." (Matthew 26:41 [NIV])

Peter ended up denying Jesus three times. If he had been alert and in prayer, perhaps he would have been able to resist the temptation to betray Jesus.

Peter wasn't the only one; many people fell into temptations in the Bible. That's why it's been recorded—for our learning. The sin of sexual immorality is especially frequent. Tamar, Judah's daughter-in-law, disguised herself as a prostitute to sleep with her father-in-law and get pregnant.[9] King David

---

8   https://bible.org/seriespage/q-how-do-you-tell-test-temptation
9   Genesis 38

sinned when he lusted over Bathsheba, Uriah's wife, which led to adultery and ultimately, murder.[10]

Sin fascinates before it assassinates. A literal example of the power of sin to assassinate is Judas. After betraying Jesus with a kiss for 30 pieces of silver, which was somewhere between $91 to $441 in present-day value (USD), he committed suicide.

It is extremely important to **pray** so when the temptations come—and they will—you do not fall into them.

Prioritize a Pure Heart

I've had my share of temptations as well. As a teenager, I fell into the temptation of masturbation.

What began my deliverance was when I found the lists of things God hates: "...a proud look, a lying tongue, and hands that shed innocent blood, **a heart that deviseth wicked imaginations**, feet that be swift in running to mischief, a false witness that speaketh lies, and he that soweth discord among brethren." (Proverbs 6:16-19 [KJV])

I didn't think God could hate things, but He does. God hates sin, especially sin against our bodies, which are meant to be a dwelling place for His spirit.

Ask God for Guidance

With a deep revelation of the word HATE, I prayed what I considered my greatest prayer ever prayed at that time. I asked God to make me hate the things He hates. The fact is God hates sin, especially sin against our bodies because our bodies are God's temple. The sin of the body separates us from God. That's why Apostle Paul urges us to "flee from sexual immorality. All other sins a person commits are outside the body, but whoever sins sexually, sins against their own body." (1 Corinthians 6:18 [NIV])

After continuously praying and desiring freedom, I lost the desire to masturbate—but the devil wasn't done with me.

After some years, I realized the devil began to tempt me with impure thoughts. I would sit down and unholy thoughts would begin to fill my mind. Indeed, an idle mind is the devil's workshop, and Satan was carrying out his duties very well.

Again, I had to go to God for deliverance, but this time, it wasn't easy. It required my participation in "casting down imaginations, and every high thing that exalteth itself against the knowledge of God, and bringing into captivity every thought to the obedience of Christ." (2 Corinthians 10:5 [KJV])

In my journey to sexual purity, the Holy Spirit led me to create a 4 Weeks Eye Gate Challenge based on Luke 11:34: "Your eye is the lamp of your body. When your eyes are healthy, your whole body also is full of light. But when they are unhealthy, your body also is full of darkness."[11]

I posted this on my website for others to download the free eBook. I also shared an Instagram post asking people to join the challenge and let them know I'd be happy to serve as an accountability partner.

The post reached 4,655 people, 50.2% women and 48.4% men, and 289 people interacted with the post. I share these statistics to show you that temptation of sexual sin is not gender specific. Here's a testimony of someone who took the 4 Weeks Eye Gate Challenge:

> "I'd like to testify to how God rescued me from the shackles of death. Last year, I had some issues. Battling with my sexuality and all. I was trying to find a place and thought there was really no place for me here. Then during May or June, I got drugged and it was wild. I still remember that day and sometimes I get scared till now. I had several episodes of paranoia, trying to differentiate reality from imagination, and oh Lord, it sucked. Then I met you. God used you to help me. I prayed and then went to church that day and gradually I started becoming better. To be honest, what God cannot do really doesn't exist. God is real. The Holy Spirit is real. Thank you for being a vessel. Hallelujah."

---

11   New International Version (NIV)

Recently, the Holy Spirit gave me a revelation of how destructive sexual sin is. He took my attention to Matthew 12:43-45:

> "When an impure Spirit comes out of a person, it goes through arid places seeking rest and does not find it. Then it says, 'I will return to the house I left.' When it arrives, it finds the house unoccupied, swept clean and put in order. Then it goes and takes with it seven other spirits more wicked than itself, and they go in and live there. And the final condition of that person is worse than the first."
> —Matthew 12:43-45 (NIV)

The house containing the impure Spirit was empty, unoccupied. Jesus was no longer Lord of that house, and so it gave the impure Spirit an opportunity to gather seven more wicked spirits to torment that person, leaving them worse than the first time.

This revelation made me think of Jesus's encounter with the demon-possessed man in Luke 8:26-39: "Jesus asked him, 'What is your name?' 'Legion,' he replied, because many demons had gone into him."[12]

If you understand the gravity of allowing another Spirit other than the Holy Spirit in your body, you will not engage in sexual sin. That's why James 4:7 says it best: "Submit

---

12   New International Version (NIV)

yourselves, then, to God. Resist the devil, and he will flee from you."[13]

The temptation you are facing might be something other than sexual temptation, but nonetheless, we are to pray that we do not fall into any sort of temptation. Jesus is our best example. Jesus was tempted by the devil in the wilderness after His 40-day fast. Satan tempted Jesus with:

1. The lust of the flesh: "If you are the Son of God, tell these stones to become bread." (Matthew 4:3 [NIV])

2. The pride of life: "'If you are the Son of God,' he said, 'throw yourself down.' For it is written: 'He will command his angels concerning you, and they will lift you up in their hands, so that you will not strike your foot against a stone.'" (Matthew 4:6 [NIV])

3. The lust of the eyes: "The devil took him to a very high mountain and showed him all the kingdoms of the world and their splendor. 'All this I will give you,' he said, 'if you will bow down and worship me.'" (Matthew 4:9 [NIV])

It can be easy to discredit Jesus' temptation as He was God; however, He was in human form at the time, and thus would have felt the aftereffects of a 40-day fast. If you've ever fasted for any period of time, you know how tired and hungry you get. Now, imagine yourself without food or water for 40

---

days and someone offers you bread. Wouldn't you be quick to accept regardless of the condition attached? Esau did. He accepted bread and lentil stew in exchange for his birthright to his brother Jacob and came to regret it years later. (Genesis 25:29-34) Esau was famished, Jesus was tired, David was idle. It is often in our weak states that the devil tempts us, and unfortunately, we all have fallen into temptation at one point in our lives or another.

I know this chapter is really heavy. It was one of the most difficult chapters for me to write. However, I would not be emphasizing this if it weren't serious. Sexual sin is so serious that Jesus tells us in Matthew 5:28-30:

> "But I tell you that anyone who looks at a woman lustfully has already committed adultery with her in her heart. If your right eye causes you to stumble, gouge it out and throw it away. It is better for you to lose one part of your body than for your whole body to be thrown into hell. And if your right hand causes you to stumble, cut it off and throw it away. It is better for you to lose one part of your body than for your whole body to go into hell."[14]

This is a radical statement, but of course Jesus isn't literally saying you should cut off your arm and take out your eyes.

---

14   New International Version (NIV)

He is trying to show you the gravity of sexual immorality. It can metastasize, causing your entire body to be unhealthy.

And if you've already engaged in sexual immorality, don't beat yourself up about it. It happens to the best of us. But now that you have a better revelation of its effect, make it a priority to guard your heart and flee from it.

What Jesus Repeats We Must Revere

Jesus repeated to His disciples: "Get up and pray so that you will not give in to temptation."

The devil knows you have a bright future. He comes to tempt you with food so you become gluttonous and unhealthy so as to be unfit for the work ahead; with money so you can stop following Christ to pursue the degrees and networks that would bring you fame and money; with relationships that seem to fill the gaps in your heart so you forget the most important relationship is with Christ Jesus. To overcome temptation, you need the weapons of prayer, worship, and the Word—plus accountability partners.

Flood Your Life

In 2022, God told me, "FLOOD YOUR LIFE WITH EVERYTHING GOD."

God was saying, "Involve me in everything. I want to be in every nook and corner of your life." That's what I tried to do, and that's what God wants you to do. Whatever the object of your temptation is, Jesus asks us to pray to overcome it.

So, let us PRAY *this*:

Heavenly Father, I recognize why the devil wants to tempt me to sin. He wants to separate me from You because You are holy and cannot dwell where sin resides. I confess my sins and receive forgiveness. I pray for the power of the Holy Spirit to live above sin. Today, I take captive every thought that is not of you. I hide my heart in you, and I choose today to guard my eyes, heart, ears, and mind. I give the devil no place in my body, now and forever. In Jesus's Name. Amen.

Reflection

Listen to the song "Yield Not to Temptation" by Horatio Richmond Palmer and use the following prompts to kick off your reflection on this chapter, which you can write in the blank pages provided.

1. What temptations are you struggling with?
2. What actions can you take to flee temptation?

BELIEVE

God's Sovereignty

While we can pray for anything, it is wise to have a heart check before making our requests. This is to ensure that as we pray, we align with God's will for our lives and not pray amiss.

While getting my bachelor's degree, I was working per diem as a certified nursing assistant. I had been working in the hospital setting for two years before the Covid-19 outbreak. I had transferred from a community college to a private university after spending two years on my associate degree. I had two more years to complete my bachelor's and I was determined to finish within those two years because I was of

---

15   Hebrews 11:6 (NLT)

the opinion that no one should take more than four years to complete an undergrad degree. I was proud and arrogant, so God quickly humbled me as after four years, I was missing some courses and had to spend an extra semester even after all the summer classes I took.

Having planned to take those remaining courses in Fall 2020 and graduate, I realized I had to pay $13,451—and I did not have that kind of money. This meant I had to pause school for a semester, and it would take me 5 years to complete my degree. I was devastated. I was running like a chicken with its head cut off. I tried all avenues to get quick cash, but they all failed. Finally, I went to God in prayer. Isn't it funny how our last resort is God when He should be our first?

I ended up working through the fall of 2020, covered in personal protective equipment: gowns, masks, gloves, and face shields. It was a humbling experience, and while I waited, worked, and saved, I prayed for a miracle. I knew God had allowed this to happen to me to humble me and rely on Him.

When the spring semester approached, I checked my school registration portal and my balance was $5,951. That's a $7,500 reduction! I didn't want to know the logic behind it; I knew it was God's divine intervention.

This event turned my attention to Mark 11:24[16]: "For this reason I am telling you, whatever things you ask for in prayer [in accordance with God's will], believe [with confident trust] that you have received them, and they will be given to you."

---

16   Amplified Bible (AMP)

The key statement here is "in accordance to God's will." This is how we know our prayers must submit to the sovereignty of God.

In The Lord's Prayer, when Jesus asked us to pray, He said, "Thy will be done." This is a very important prayer to embody when we are making prayer requests because although we have desires, we must remember that God's will is to be done above all else. God will not allow something to happen to us that will not ultimately produce the fruit of the Spirit within us.

Purify the Purpose of Your Prayer

When we pray, we must be careful not to ask with the wrong motives. My initial motive for asking God to provide my tuition for the fall semester was to avoid the shame of not finishing school in exactly four years. What lesson would I have gained if God had provided the money I needed before my perspective had changed?

I later realized that once I had focused on how my degree would help *other* people, everything changed and God granted me with money towards my goal. It wasn't the complete amount, but I was extremely grateful. It wasn't about the money for me. It was about learning how to pray effectively and learning what God did or didn't want me to do. This is why it's important to pay attention to exactly *how* God grants us His blessings. God is always trying to tell us something within every detail. For this, we must remain attentive.

James 4:3 helps shed light on this issue. He says, "You ask [God for something] and do not receive it, because you ask with wrong motives [out of selfishness or with an unrighteous agenda], so that [when you get what you want] you may spend it on your [hedonistic] desires."[17]

God is more likely to answer a prayer to transform your life or character, give you boldness to share the gospel, or fill your life with peace and contentment than He is to give you all the things of this world for you to just lose your soul.

Some of us become like the rich fool when God blesses us.[18] Instead of showing gratitude to the God who blessed him, he thought to himself: "What shall I do?"

He didn't even think of giving a tenth of his harvest back to God as tithe; instead, he thought about building bigger barns to store his crops.

This is the result of not hearkening the wisdom of Proverbs 3:4-5 by leaning on our own understanding instead of acknowledging God in ALL OUR WAYS.[19]

The rich fool took it a step further: "And I'll say to myself, 'You have plenty of grain laid up for many years. Take life easy; eat, drink and be merry.'"[20]

He was boastful, arrogant, and selfish. Isn't this how many of us become at the smell of wealth, influence, and fame?

---

17   Amplified Bible (AMP)
18   Luke 12:13-21(NIV)
19   Proverbs 3:6
20   New International Version (NIV)

That night, God demanded the rich fool's life from him. The parable ends with Jesus saying: "This is how it will be with whoever stores up things for themselves but is not rich toward God."[21]

In your quest for your desires to be met, may you pray for the wisdom to seek God's will over your own. When you pray, you must pray in faith—from the start.

Jesus speaking to His disciples says, "I tell you, you can pray for anything, and if you believe that you've received it, it will be yours." (Mark 11:24 [NLT])

Brave Prayers

In Mark Batterson's book, *Whisper*, he talks about the bravest prayer he ever prayed: that God would heal his asthma. It was a brave prayer because a life with debilitating asthma was all he'd ever known. He defined a brave prayer as "the prayer you can barely believe God for because it seems impossible. It's often the prayer you've prayed a hundred times that hasn't been answered, but you pray it one more time anyway."

Mark had prayed hundreds of prayers to be healed from asthma and had his prayers go unanswered. He recounts a moment before his freshman year of high school. He had been hospitalized for a severe asthma attack in the intensive care unit. After he was released, a pastor and his prayer team came over to Mark's home, laid hands on him and prayed that God would heal his asthma—and even then he was not

---

21   New International Version (NIV)

healed. Despite this, Mark writes, "God answered that prayer for healing but not in a way I expected."

God had answered the prayer of healing by removing all the warts on his feet, showing Mark that He is able. This small but significant miracle increased Mark's faith to believe that God could heal his asthma, so he kept praying.

God healed Mark after four decades of living with asthma. This shows that delay is not denial. God hears you and will answer at the right time. It might not be the right time for you, but God is never late and is always on time. Peter reminds us, "But do not forget this one thing, dear friends: With the Lord a day is like a thousand years, and a thousand years are like a day." (2 Peter 3:14 [NIV])

Hey, nugget! Yes, you! God is able! He may not answer in the way you expect, but if you take time to count your blessings and the many small daily miracles, it will strengthen you to keep praying. I love what Matthew 7:7 says: "Keep on asking, and you will receive what you ask for. Keep on seeking, and you will find. Keep on knocking, and the door will be opened to you."[22]

---

22   New Living Translation (NLT)

So, let us PRAY *this*:

Heavenly Father, I have come to realize that even when I believe, I also have doubts, like the father with the mute child in Mark 9:24. Help me to see you in the many daily miracles and to believe that you are able. Please strengthen my faith that as I pray in accordance to your will, that it will be done. In Jesus's Name. Amen.

Reflection

Listen to the song "Believe For It" by CeCe Winans and use the following prompts to kick off your reflection on this chapter, which you can write in the blank pages provided.

1. What or who did you stop praying for because you did not receive the answers you wanted at the time you needed them?

2. How does God's sovereignty influence your prayers?

HARDSHIPS

Hardship is a ship you don't want to be in. Nobody wants to experience the hard knocks of life. We all dream of and pursue a life of constant comfort and pleasure. Unfortunately, that is not reality. At many points in our lives, we will face things that are difficult to endure.[23] James tells us that in times of hardships, our first response should be to pray this: "Are any of you suffering hardships? You should pray." (James 5:13 [NLT])

A hard ship to be on is when a family member is gravely ill. This is a challenging time, and it can leave you powerless, but there is a solution. James says: "Is anyone among you sick? Let them call the elders of the church to pray over them and anoint them with oil in the name of the Lord. And the prayer offered in faith will make the sick person well; the Lord will raise them up. If they have sinned, they will be forgiven." (James 5:14-15 [NIV])

---

23   John 16:33

Prayer Is the Antidote to Hardships

I always love hearing healing testimonies because it proves that miracles still happen. It perplexes me that when people are sick, they hide it from the church. I considered that the fear and shame of going through the disease overwhelms them. They might begin to think, "What will people say when they hear this?" In fact, we see this in the scriptures.

In John 9, Jesus and His disciples meet a man blind from birth. If you notice in scripture, most people who were sick, male or female, were addressed by their illness, not their name. It is not uncommon for people to name you after your illness. "Oh, the woman who has cancer," and forget your name. The disease immediately becomes your identity, just like this man was termed "blind from birth."

The disciples who went on to become elders and pioneers of the first church leading the first Christians asked the question, "Rabbi, who sinned, this man or his parents, that he was born blind?" This is such an interesting question. The question assumes that for a person to be with such illness that he or someone close to him must have sinned. How many times have we thought that what someone was going through was due to his or her own fault? The person was reaping all the bad deeds they sowed, and we were thus pleased with the result.

Jesus said to His disciples, "Neither this man nor his parents sinned…but this happened so that the works of God might be displayed in him." (John 9:3 [NIV])

Pray for Miracles

One scripture that comes to mind when the topic of sickness is brought up is Isaiah 38. In this chapter, "Hezekiah became ill and was at the point of death," and prophet Isaiah said, "Put your house in order, because you are going to die; you will not recover."[24]

I love what Hezekiah did even after receiving the bad news from the prophet Isaiah: "Hezekiah turned his face to the wall and prayed to the Lord,"[25] and the bearer of bad news became the bearer of good news.

The Lord sent Isaiah back to Hezekiah with the good news: "I have heard your prayer and seen your tears; I will add fifteen years to your life. And I will deliver you and this city from the hand of the king of Assyria. I will defend this city."

Isn't this awesome? Now that's a miracle! The story of Hezekiah should push us to pray when gravely ill—or even just sick. As you pray, search the scriptures for healing passages and confess them daily. Invite the elders of the church and let an altar of intercession be built on your behalf.

24   New International Version (NIV)
25   New International Version (NIV)

Anointing with Oil

The latter part of this verse talks about anointing with oil, which is important. There's a reel going around—you've probably seen it—that depicts growing up with a prayerful mom waking her children up in the middle of the night to pray and anoint them with oil. I live that life, and I'm grateful to have parents who have been a spiritual covering for me throughout my life.

At times, I did not understand the reason and dismissed their efforts, but as I grow older and search the scriptures for myself, I see the importance of obeying the scriptures by anointing with oil—even if it seems like a foolish thing to do. In the Old Testament, the anointing of oil was used to ordain priests who entered into God's holy place on behalf of the Israelites, and to appoint kings as we see in 2 Samuel 5:3 where David was anointed by Samuel to take over leadership from Saul, but it is more than that.

Isaiah 10:27 states: "...his burden shall be taken away from off thy shoulder, and his yoke from off thy neck, and the yoke shall be destroyed because of the anointing."[26] The anointing has yoke-destroying power. A yoke is a wooden crosspiece that is fastened over the necks of two animals and attached to the plow or cart that they are to pull. Spiritually, a yoke means attachment, entanglement, and bondage. Anointing has the power to break the yoke.

---

26   King James Version (KJV)

The oil itself has no effect without God's Spirit. This is evinced by God's Spirit being on Paul; it was so powerful that even his clothes still healed people.[27] That's what makes the difference—the presence of God's Spirit is what causes the anointing oil to transcend the physical and become spiritual yoke destroyer.

Take a trip to the store today and purchase a bottle of oil. Sometimes spiritual things can sound foolish, but I would rather be a fool for Christ than wise in my own self. Now, deciding against this practice does not make you less of a Christian, but if James writes about it, then I think we ought to consider it.

We Can't Tell the Future, So Pray

We can have nest eggs and all sorts of plans to prevent hardships, but the truth is no one can ever really anticipate the magnitude of hardships. We never anticipated the pandemic in 2019 that led to so many deaths and long-term effects. We never anticipated inflation and the loss of jobs. We never anticipated the rise of individuals needing mental health care.

So, how do you prepare for the trouble of this world? Whenever you are faced with a hardship of any sort, your first instinct should be to pray. Talk to Jesus about it and wait to listen to what He has to say.

Hardships really are like ships; they always have a destination. When you are on that ship, it is for a reason. Don't be

---

27   Acts 19:11-12

in a hurry to get out on the lifeboat and paddle back. Stay on the ship and allow God to navigate. You will get to your destination!

So, let us PRAY *this*:

Heavenly Father, thank you for the many hardships in my life. Although I have resisted them, they have made me stronger and better in the long run. Please help me to see hardship as a way to get closer to You. May I turn to You first in prayer whenever I am faced with hardships. Help me to persevere through hard times as You guide me to the other side. Help me to search your Word for healing promises and to pray in faith that I am healed. In Jesus's Name. AMEN.

Reflection

Listen to the song "Can't Give Up Now" by Mary Mary and use the following prompts to kick off your reflection on this chapter, which you can write in the blank pages provided.

1. What is something hard you are going through?

2. How can you cultivate perseverance through hard times?

PRAY FOR THE INTERPRETATION OF TONGUES

"So anyone who speaks in tongues should pray also for the ability to interpret what has been said."
-1 Corinthians 14:13 (NLT)

S peaking in tongues is evidence and a gift for everyone who receives Christ Jesus as Lord and Savior. The earliest record of someone speaking in tongues is in Acts 2:

"When the day of Pentecost came, they were all together in one place. Suddenly a sound like the blowing of a violent wind came from heaven and filled the whole house where they were sitting. They saw what seemed to be tongues of fire that separated and came to rest on each of them. All of them were filled with the Holy Spirit and began to speak in other tongues as the Spirit enabled them."[28]

The dumbfounding (to the onlookers) part of this was that the people in the upper room were all Galileans, but being

---

28   New International Version (NIV)

filled with the Holy Spirit, they burst into tongues, and God-fearing Jews from every nation under heaven in Jerusalem began to hear the wonders of God in their native languages. This included the Parthians, Medes, and Elamites; residents of Mesopotamia, Judea and Cappadocia, Pontus and Asia, Phrygia and Pamphylia, Egypt and the parts of Libya near Cyrene; visitors from Rome (both Jews and converts to Judaism); Cretans and Arabs!

This scripture can be compared to the story of the tower of Babel in which people who all spoke one language said to themselves, "Come, let us build ourselves a city, with a tower that reaches to the heavens, so that we may make a name for ourselves; otherwise we will be scattered over the face of the whole earth" (Genesis 11:4 [NIV]).

These people were so aligned in their purpose that nothing could stop them...except for a language barrier. "So the Lord scattered them from there over all the earth, and they stopped building the city. That is why it was called Babel—because there the Lord confused the language of the whole world. From there the Lord scattered them over the face of the whole earth." (Genesis 11:7-9 [NIV])

Babylon brought confusion, and many years later, the Holy Spirit brought understanding. In Babylon, people were scattered because of language, and in Jerusalem, people were brought together as they listened to the apostles teach in their own language as inspired by the Holy Spirit. Isn't that amazing?

The Beauty of Speaking in Tongues

I was blessed to have started speaking in tongues at the age of twelve. One evening, we had just finished a service my mom had preached. When we arrived home, she called my older sister and I to the sitting room and began laying her hands on us and praying.

She was quoting scriptures like, "Whoever believes in me, as Scripture has said, rivers of living water will flow from within them," (John 7:38) and "I am the Lord thy God, which brought thee out of the land of Egypt: open thy mouth wide, and I will fill it" (Psalms 81:10).

Suddenly, as I opened my mouth, what sounded like gibberish began to spew and I could not control it. Over time, that gibberish has grown into praying in tongues and a private understanding of the Holy Spirit's utterance through me, which should not be confused with the gift of the public interpretation of tongues.

When I struggle to pray, the Holy Spirit makes intercession on my behalf. As I begin to speak in tongues, things that I wanted to pray about but had no words for become clear to me and it feels like I'm saying it but in a spiritual language known to God.

1 Corinthians 2:10-12 explains the interpretation of tongues best:

"These are the things God has revealed to us by his Spirit. The Spirit searches all things, even the deep things of God. For who knows a person's thoughts except their own Spirit within them? In the same way, no one knows the thoughts of God except the Spirit of God. What we have received is not the Spirit of the world, but the Spirit who is from God, that we may understand what God has freely given us."[29]

This Gift Is Available to All

My prayer is that you be baptized with the language of tongues because it's such an awesome way to communicate with God. However, there are some misconceptions about speaking in tongues, so I would like to clarify some things:

You do not need to speak in tongues or be able to interpret tongues to be saved and go to heaven.

Those who speak in tongues and/or have the gift of interpretation are not more mature than believers who don't.

Once you are saved, the presence of the Holy Spirit lives inside of you.

Speaking in tongues is for any believer who wants to experience it. Pray and ask God for a manifestation of the Holy Spirit in your life through speaking in tongues and their interpretation.

---

29   New International Version (NIV)

Speaking in tongues gives us a supernatural voice that amplifies our voice and strengthens our authority on earth. It gives us the boldness to spread the gospel to glorify Christ. Next time you're praying, pause and ask for the gift of speaking in tongues. Paul in Romans 8:26 tells us that "likewise the Spirit also helpeth our infirmities: for we know not what we should pray for as we ought: but the Spirit itself maketh intercession for us with groanings which cannot be uttered."[30] Speaking in tongues is a gift from God and Paul in Ephesians 6:18 urges us to "pray in the Spirit at all times and on every occasion."[31]

Who Is the Holy Spirit?

You need the Holy Spirit. He is not just a feeling, a voice, a dove, or your conscience, although, these are forms of His expression; He is one third of the trinity. He is the Spirit of God. The issue is that most times we're seeking the gifts of the Spirit without seeking the giver – God himself.

John 14:26 speaks of the Holy Spirit as an advocate to teach you all things and remind you of everything Jesus had spoken of. The Holy Spirit is here to stay with us forever; He lives with you. (John 14:16-17) John 16:13 speaks of Him as a guide into all truth; not speaking on his own but only what he hears from our Father, telling us what is to come.

It is that same Spirit that produces in us love, joy, peace, patience, kindness, goodness, faithfulness, gentleness, and

---

30   King James Version (KJV)
31   New International Version (NIV)

self-control. (Galatians 5:22-24 [NIV]) If we truly walk by the Spirit, we will not gratify the desires of the flesh. (Galatians 5:16 [NIV]) If we truly allow our minds to be governed by the Spirit, we will have life and peace (Romans 8:6)

Most importantly, it is the Holy Spirit that gives us the power to do kingdom work. "But you will receive power when the Holy Spirit comes on you; and you will be my witnesses in Jerusalem, and in all Judea and Samaria, and to the ends of the earth." (Acts 1:8 [NIV]). Without the power of the Holy Spirit, we can still do kingdom work, but it wouldn't be Spirit-led—and Spirit-led kingdom work is the most effective. It is the Holy Spirit that makes the difference, so let us seek to solidify our relationship with the Holy Spirit.

So, let us PRAY *this*:

Heavenly Father, I come to You today longing for the gift of speaking in tongues and interpreting tongues, but first, I want Your Spirit to dwell richly in me. Holy Spirit of the living God, I ask that you fill my heart, lead me, guide me, teach me, and empower me to live a life above sin and to proclaim the gospel of Christ Jesus. In Jesus's Name. Amen.

Reflection

Listen to the song "Holy Spirit" by Jesus Culture and use the following prompts to kick off your reflection on this chapter, which you can write in the blank pages provided.

1. What is your experience with speaking in tongues and/or the interpretation of tongues?

2. How has being filled with the Holy Spirit impacted your life?

THE LORD'S PRAYER

(Matthew 6:9-13)[32]

One of the most popular prayers in the Bible is The Lord's Prayer. Alongside Psalms 23, you probably memorized it as a child. My aim in this chapter is to take each line and expand on it to enable you to observe closely each word, reflect on its meaning, and extract the maximum benefit from it.

"Our Father who art in heaven"

The Ultimate Father Figure

I love that Jesus first starts this prayer with addressing God as "our Father." Coming from the Old Testament where some of our interpretation of God is that He is cold and hard to please to the New Testament where God is introduced to us as "our Father" is very impactful.

In the Old Testament, the law was just for the Israelites, but in the New Testament, Jesus came to all people (the Greeks, the Samaritans…). "Our Father" is much more approachable than "GOD." Yes, God is still God, but through Jesus's work on the cross, we all now have direct access to our Father without having to have a priest atone for our sins with animal sacrifices.

God is your Father in heaven. Unfortunately, if you had or have an unhealthy relationship with your earthly father, when you approach our Father in heaven, your view of Him may be skewed by your relationship with your earthly father. It is vital to recognize that God did not hurt you, cannot hurt you, and will never hurt you. Your Heavenly Father is not your earthly father, and in learning more about your Heavenly Father, you learn about yourself and how to become better at showing the love of Christ to all people.

"hallowed be your name" (Matthew 6:9)

Worship Paves the Way

When we come into God's presence to seek His face, we must first worship Him. Oftentimes, people approach our Father murmuring about that supervisor that's giving them a headache or their kids pressing their buttons. I approach God for grace to ace my classes because I don't want to repeat them, and for patience to work through relationship issues. While all these wants and needs are perfectly valid, it is not how you should begin to pray.

Jesus started His prayer by honoring God's name: "This, then, is how you should pray: 'Our Father in heaven, hallowed be your name.'" Likewise, it is important that when we begin our prayer to our Heavenly Father that we approach Him with a heart posture of worship, praise, adoration, thanksgiving, and rejoicing.

Our flesh is mostly selfish, so we need to be intentional in playing or singing a song to create an atmosphere of thanksgiving. I often wake up singing new songs that God places in my heart, and it allows me to easily flow into my time of prayer. The YouVersion app has a prayer section with instrumentals to choose from that create an atmosphere of thanksgiving as you pray.

"your kingdom come, your will be done, on earth as it is in heaven" (**Matthew 6:10**)

I once heard a pastor define the word "earth" in this verse as us—you and me—and it helped me look at this prayer differently.

God's Will in You

In Genesis 2:7, "the Lord God formed man of the dust of the ground, and breathed into his nostrils the breath of life, and man became a living soul."[33] Our bodies are earthen vessels made of dust.

The reason God created man and woman and "blessed them and said to them, 'Be fruitful and increase in number; fill the earth and subdue it,'" was to create more earthen vessels where His Spirit can dwell.

As you say The Lord's Prayer, I not only want you to think of God's will being done on planet Earth, but also in you, the earthen vessel, as He planned from the beginning.

"Give us today our daily bread." (Matthew 6:11)

Tithe, Sow, Eat, Give

"Bread" is what we need to survive. As a spiritual being in an earthen vessel, you need the bread of life, which is God's Word, to sustain your spiritual life.

Jesus's comeback to Satan after being tempted to turn stone into bread was, "Man shall not live by bread alone, but by every word that comes from the mouth of God."[34]

Another way to think of the word "bread" is as seed. God graciously meets our needs daily, just like He provided manna

---

33   King James Version (KJV)
34   English Standard Version (ESV)

for the Israelites in the wilderness. However, God also gives seed to the sower.[35] Hence, it is safe to say that if you do not have enough, then maybe you should check your giving meter.

Luke 6:38 says: "Give, and it will be given to you. A good measure, pressed down, shaken together and running over, will be poured into your lap. For with the measure you use, it will be measured to you."[36]

For you to eat and have enough to give, you need to be a good steward of God's blessings. The problem is that a lot of us eat our seed for immediate reward only to suffer in the long term.

Also, when God blesses you and you have abundance, you are not supposed to hoard it. The parable of the rich fool in Luke 12:13-21 that we explored in the previous chapter tells us that when God gives you your daily bread, be sure to not only store it, but also tithe, sow, eat, and give.

"And forgive us our debts, as we also have forgiven our debtors" **(Matthew 6:12)**

Forgiveness

This has an interesting format. It simply says, "forgive me because I have forgiven," meaning you need to forgive before you are forgiven. Forgiveness is not optional for the believer. It is a way of life and is important to do before praying.

Jesus in Mark 11:25-26 says: "Whenever you stand praying, if you have anything against anyone, forgive him [drop the issue, let it go], so that your Father who is in heaven will also forgive you your transgressions and wrongdoings [against Him and others]. [But if you do not forgive, neither will your Father in heaven forgive your transgressions.]"[37]

God cares more about your heart and relationships with others than He does your tithes, offerings, and extravagant giving. Yes, those are great too, but we need to have good relationships in order to grow and spread the gospel of Christ.

The truth of the matter is that many times in your life, you will be offended. Offenses will come, but what matters is what you choose to do with that offense. You have two options: hold onto it or let it go; neither are easy, but the latter is freeing.

Forgiveness is the very act of letting go. It is not ignoring and moving on. It is acknowledging the hurt and still choosing to let go of the idea of vengeance. Forgiveness looks like praying for those who hurt you. What forgiveness does not look like is sweeping it under the rug and never deciding to address the issue. The more you continue to sweep hurts under the rug and ignore them, the more likely you are to one day trip over them.

---

37   Amplified Bible (AMP)

How do you know if you haven't forgiven? Simple: when the thought of that person arises or the name of the person is mentioned anywhere close to you, take notice of how you feel in that moment. Where do your thoughts go? Do you wish for vengeance? Does your heart beat fast and do your hands round in a fist? Well, then, you still have some work to do.

Forgive Yourself

It is easier to forgive others when you forgive yourself, but most of us fail miserably at forgiving ourselves. We're our own worst critics. Know that God has already provided a way of forgiveness and it's up to you to receive it.

In Matthew 8:21, Peter asked Jesus a wonderful question about forgiveness: "Lord, how often should I forgive someone who sins against me? Seven times?" Jesus answered and said, "No, not seven times, but seventy times seven!"[38]

That's 490 times! I'm sure no one is able to keep record of the number of times someone offends them and they forgive, but even if you are, the basis of Jesus saying this was not to provide the maximum forgiveness number. It is in fact a hyperbole, which is often used in the Bible. Forgiveness has no limit. "Freely you have received; freely give." (Matthew 10:8 [NIV])

As therapy increases and people are more conscious of their mental and emotional health, I understand the need to keep

---

38 New Living Translation (NLT)

some people, including family members, at a distance. Chude Jideonwo says there are two types of people:

1. People who are malevolent. They intentionally do not abide by Romans 12:15: "Rejoice with those who rejoice, weep with those who weep."[39] They lack empathy. These people consciously bring harm and are not likely to repent for their actions. It's important to remember that most people are not like this.

2. People who don't wish to hurt you—which is most people. They don't wish you harm, but they might just not know how to recognize how their actions can cause harm. These people, on the other hand, can be reasoned with once they have been made to understand or have learned their lesson.

It is important to distinguish between these two types of people. The malevolent you should keep away from. The unconscious you should guide and correct, and sometimes over and over again—start with 490 times! You know they're not coming from a bad place but rather a lack of understanding and experience.

In Luke 23, when Christ was on the cross, He prayed to His Father, "Please forgive them for they do not know what they're doing."[40] That's different from the language used to

---

39   English Standard Version (ESV)
40   New International Version (NIV)

address the religious leaders in Matthew 23 who thought Jesus was the source of their problems and there to prevent the Jews from obeying the laws of Moses, thus believing they needed to crucify Him.

He called them "brood of vipers," "blind guides," "hypocrites."[41] By example, Jesus teaches us that it is important to be discerning but also forgiving because human beings are imperfect. We say and do things we shouldn't. If we reject everybody who says something to us we don't like, we will not have any friends and we will go deeper into judging ourselves because we will soon realize that we ourselves are imperfect.

Find those who are unconscious contributors of headaches in your life. Hold them responsible. Tell them what they did that you don't like. Give them the space and room to do better and to try to stop being unconscious. We are each responsible for our own actions.

Paul in Hebrews 12:14 says to "follow peace with all men, and holiness, without which no man shall see the Lord."[42] Let us learn to be peaceful in our dealings with each other, even if we don't agree on all matters. Your greatest enemy is the devil, not your neighbor or someone from a different political party from yours.

"And lead us not into temptation"

Revisit the chapter on "Temptations" for review.

---

41   New King James Version (NKJV)
42   King James Version (KJV)

"but deliver us from evil" (Matthew 6:13)

Your greatest enemy is the devil, and if you don't think so, then he has won in deceiving you. It seems like evil has found its home in our world today. The news is full of it, and quite frankly, I'm not shocked at all. Revelations 12:12b says: "But woe to the earth and the sea, because the devil has gone down to you! He is filled with fury, because he knows that his time is short."[43]

Jesus asked us to pray that God deliver us from ALL evil— not some, but ALL. This shows the gravity of evil, but we have a God that is good and has already conquered evil, and "despite all these things, overwhelming victory is ours through Christ, who loved us." (Romans 8:37 [NLT]) We are conquerors as well in Christ Jesus.

---

43   King James Version (KJV)

Reflection

Listen to the song "The Lord's Prayer (feat. Phil Thompson)" by Jubilee Worship and use the following prompts to kick off your reflection on this chapter, which you can write in the blank pages provided.

1. How does viewing God as your Heavenly Father influence your approach to prayer?

2. What are some words you use to describe God?

3. How do you feel about your body as an earthen vessel for God's will to be done in and through?

4. Who do you need to forgive today?

PRAYERS FOR OTHERS AND THINGS BIGGER THAN YOURSELF

"She opens her hand to the poor and reaches out her hands to the needy. She is not afraid of snow for her household, for all her household are clothed in scarlet."

-Psalms 31:20-21 (ESV)

In Part 1, we covered prayers for you. In Part 2 we are going to be focusing on intercessory prayers, which are simply prayers for others and things bigger than yourself. These prayer topics are not an exhaustive list of all the things we should be praying for but rather serve as a springboard for you to delve into the Bible and find the little hidden prayer nuggets that speak to all that you are navigating in life right now.

You may be wondering, "Why do I need to pray for others when I have so many issues of my own? Someone should be praying for me!" We've all been there. We've all thought this at one time or another, but the irony of that statement is that praying for others is so powerful that it actually takes your focus off your personal worries. It develops compassion in you for others. It refocuses your attention on Jesus, the author and finisher of our faith.[44]

If you can't do anything about a certain situation, pray and believe that God will answer, and you can rest assured that Jesus is also praying for you.[45]

---

44   Hebrews 12:2
45   John 17:9 (NIV)

PRAY FOR YOUR PASTORS

Every week, I receive an email from my senior pastor. It not only has updates and announcements about the goings-on of the congregation, but it also includes a call to pray for him as he delivers his message on Sunday. I found this call to prayer interesting—and also highly necessary.

You might be wondering, "Why do *I* need to pray for my pastors? Aren't *they* the ones who are supposed to be praying for me?"

As the pastor's kid, I have taken a front row seat to the many battles my parents fought when starting a church and leading the members, many of which they protected us from and didn't share. The truth is that pastors are *human*. Yes, they live in service to His church, which is you and me, but holding the office of a pastor does not exempt them from the darts of the devil—even though God in His infinite mercy provides protection. Pastors are human vessels with God's anointing in service to His church; they are not SUPERHEROES.

Pray That Pastors Preach God's Word

Have you ever attended a service and not understood what the pastor was preaching? Although this could happen for a number of reasons, like an unready heart or pride, it could also be because the pastor is speaking from the flesh and not God's Word.

While we should be like the Berean Christians who after service, went home and did their own studying to run the pastor's message through the lens of the Bible,[46] it is also important that our pastors continue to preach God's Word and not their thoughts. The preacher not purely delivering God's Word often results in a new believer not being able to discern the Truth from opinion, which may impede their taking action to properly feed their spirit.

Aside from praying for us, our pastors should deliver God's Word clearly. Therefore, we need to pray for our pastors as a whole; for their mental health, marriages, finances, health and children. The position of a pastor is not impervious to temptation; hence, we must do our part in supporting them through prayers.

46   Acts 17:11

James Said It Best

This realization about the humanness of pastors is not a reason to fret or give up hope. There are many leaders who still stand and are restoring those who fell back to right standing. While we the body of Christ may see such falling in our midst, we should not be swift to condemn; remember that a righteous man falleth seven times, yet he rises.[47] Also, this is a caution to those who are called or chosen to leadership roles in the church. To those in seminary or pursuing a ministerial degree with the goal of one day leading a church, listen to the words of James:

> "Not many [of you] should become teachers [serving in an official teaching capacity], my brothers and sisters, for you know that we [who are teachers] will be judged by a higher standard [because we have assumed greater accountability and more condemnation if we teach incorrectly]. For we all stumble and sin in many ways. If anyone does not stumble in what he says [never saying the wrong thing], he is a perfect man [fully developed in character, without serious flaws], able to bridle his whole body and rein in his entire nature [taming his human faults and weaknesses]."
> —James 3:1-2 (AMP)

---

47   Proverbs 24:16

I do not share this verse to incite fear to the point of quitting. Wanting to pursue a life in service to God in full-time ministry is applaudable. What James is saying here is that the role of a pastor should be taken seriously. It is not for clout, fame, respect, or money. It is a position in total surrender to God's authority. You speak only what God says. You are not all of a sudden above God's commandments because you have the title Pastor, Reverend, Minister, Bishop or Archbishop.

Being a pastor's kid and seeing a possibility of ministry in the future even if I have fought against it, one prayer I make certain to pray is: "Holy Spirit chastise me before it's too late." I don't want to be blind to the little foxes of pride, arrogance, insecurity, and lust that spoil the vine.[48]

My local church does a great job of providing prayer cards with our pastors' pictures on them. We have a couple on our home fridge, and I personally have one on my cork board in my room facing my work desk. Whenever I look at a prayer card, I try my best to pray as the Holy Spirit leads.

If you have a prayer card, remember that they are not just for decorating your refrigerator. They exist for you to pray when you see them, and there is no better opportunity than these moments for you to pray for each of your leaders, calling out their names.

---

48   Solomon 2:15

So, let us PRAY *this*:

Heavenly Father, we pray for the shepherds You've placed above us to provide guidance and nurture us in faith. We know the devil is coming against their homes, peace of mind, health, finances, and all that You have blessed them with. So, as Paul in 1 Thessalonians 5:25 urged the brethren to pray for them, today we lift each and every one of our leaders (say their names). We pray for strength to overcome temptations. We pray for health to continue the work. In Jesus's Name. Amen.

Reflection

Listen to the song "The Blessing" by Cody Carnes, Elevation Worship, and Kari Jobe and use the following prompt to kick off your reflection on this chapter, which you can write in the blank pages provided.

1. How can you be a blessing to your pastors today?

PRAY FOR THOSE WHO PERSECUTE YOU

"Pray for those who persecute you."
-Matthew 5:44b (AMP)

When you hear the word *hurt*, who comes to mind?

We Hurt and Are Hurt by the Ones We Love the Most

One person who comes to my mind is my mom. My mom is an anointed prayer warrior among many other things. People often mistake me for her because I am a spitting image. I adored my mom growing up so much that I wanted to be a social worker just like her. She was strong and exuded a sense of "I've got this." Then, something changed my feelings towards her when I was 14.

I had my first relationship at 14. It was a non-sexual relationship; just chats, laughs, and food. One night, while we were messaging each other, my mom burst into my room and caught me unawares. She was pissed and took my phone. She and my dad did not want to talk about it until after the annual Women's Conference that weekend. So, I tried to stay out of their way until I was called upon.

The weekend felt like months as I awaited my verdict. Once the conference was over, I was summoned and my mom and dad spoke words that stuck with me for a decade. The words hurt. Like Jentenzen Franklin said in his book, *Love Like You've Never Been Hurt*, "Family provides us with life's greatest joys and at times life's deepest sorrows."

Don't Become What Hurt You

The words my parents spoke lingered in my heart until I heard other words that began to change my feelings towards my parents. In 2018, I attended a young adults retreat my local church set up. It was an opportunity to get away from the house and my parents—and I desired it.

Doctor Barry Young was the guest speaker for the conference, and he said something I would never forget: "**Don't become what hurt you.**" It felt like Jesus had taken down the walls of anger and resentment towards my parents and filled my heart with His love.

While it was certainly important for me to process my pain in order to heal, Jesus showed me that choosing to heal on my own time was actually rebellion. Most times, we get too comfortable with our hurts and they become normal, so we have excuses for the anger, outburts, disrespect and pain we cause the offender or unrelated parties.

The Problem with Harboring Hurt

Pain has a way of affecting everything around you. Because I was hurt, I began to unintentionally hurt people. My hurt manifested in anger and resentment towards my parents and distrust in friendships. My relationships, especially with my younger brothers, began to suffer. I had become what hurt me.

When we're hurt, we fight against the authority that hurt us, be it the church, government, parents, friends, or caregivers.

It is said that hurt people hurt people. So, I would like to ask you: who hurt you? If you have held onto harsh words spoken over you or actions taken against you, it is time to let it all go.

God made me aware that when I act out of hurt, I am hurting a child of God even if they hurt me first. When you hold on to past hurts, you lock yourself in a prison and throw away the key to freedom. Jesus wants to set you free, but you have a role to play in your freedom. You have to let go of the hurt and forgive.

You Have the Power to Unbind Yourself from Hurt

The funny thing about this event that I had stitched into the story of my life was that my mom didn't even remember what she said and thankfully, our relationship has become better as I've grown.

You've been there. You say something out of anger and don't even remember what you said. It was ironic that I held on to words my mom didn't even remember saying. That's how the devil keeps you bound in hurt—by tempting you to hyper-focus on all the details that will prove to others you've been persecuted, but you do not need this validation. God knows what you've been through and is already out there advocating for you.

The Hidden Agenda of Not Forgiving

Along my journey to forgiveness, I realized that my anger was all a conspiracy. Look out for the deliberate ways in which the devil tries to block your blessings. For example, the goal of the enemy is to destroy the family unit and turn children against their parents. If children are in disunity with their parents, they cannot fulfill the fifth commandment and will therefore miss out on the blessing of long life: "Honor your father and your mother, that your days may be long in the land that the Lord your God is giving you." (Exodus 20:12 [NLT])

The Direct Path to Letting Go

The most effective way to let go is to pray for those who hurt you. The act of spreading love completely neutralizes the spreading of pain. Although therapy has helped me work through my feelings towards my mom and dad, praying for them was the catalyst that transformed my relationship with them. When I began to pray for my parents, I felt God's love fill my heart. I was no longer filled with hatred and resentment, and my relationship with my brothers was restored.

As in the song "Closer" by Mezzo Piano, Jesus pulled me a little closer and wrapped His loving arms around me. His love ravished my heart, took me over, took me deeper, and showed me the plan He had for me. He told me that I was not a disgrace but graced, and I was not disowned but adopted into the family of God. With that overflowing love, I learned to love those who hurt me, for "we love because He first loved us."[49]

I love particularly how the NLV translation puts it: "Pray for those who do bad things to you and who make it hard for you." (Matthew 5:44b)

---

49   1 John 4:19 (NIV)

So, let us **PRAY** *this*:

Heavenly Father, I am hurt, sad, and broken for the words spoken over me and the actions done against me. My actions and words reflect past hurt and hurt others. Your Word says in Matthew 5:44b that I should pray for those who do bad things to me and who make it hard for me. Today, I pray for (insert name). I ask that You show them how much You love them. If they are harboring any hurt, please heal their heart. May they not become what hurt them. And Lord, I pray for myself that Your love heals all hurt. Teach me to love out of Your love for me. In Jesus's Name. Amen.

Reflection

Listen to the song "Free" by Kierra Sheard and use the following prompts to kick off your reflection on this chapter, which you can write in the blank pages provided.

1. How has holding on to past hurts negatively impacted your life?

2. What is something you have to let go of?

PRAY FOR LABORERS

One day, I was watching Christine Cain's video series, *Best Work* (which inspired this book!), and in the first episode, she talks about how the Greeks do not like to work and love their afternoon naps, which contributed to the country's recession. It was interesting to listen to her story, especially amidst a season of worker shortage in America.

In Matthew 9, we are made aware of a shortage of workers in the kingdom of God. Jesus "was moved with compassion" when He saw the multitude "because they fainted, and were scattered abroad, as sheep having no shepherd." He spoke to His disciples: "The harvest is great, but the workers are few. So pray to the Lord who is in charge of the harvest; ask him to send more workers into his fields." (Luke 10:2 [NLT])

Service Is an Investment with a Reward

I am honored to serve on my local church's worship team. One summer, we were asked to block out the dates that we could not serve. I blocked out three Sundays I could not serve due to legit reasons, but then I went on and blocked four more Sundays. My excuse was I was taking a 6-week summer course and wanted balance. I even made excuses not to go to DIG, my young adults weekly night meeting, because I was tired.

"But not too tired to watch TV, right?" God chastised[50] me.

At the time, I used to love to come back home from a long workday and chill on my couch watching TV and having dinner. God told me if I would stop watching movies, I would have more time to spend in His presence where He would strengthen me for His work.[51]

I felt exposed. Isn't it funny how God gets all up in your business? He wasn't lying, though (He never does!). It was true! At the time, my schedule was simple. Wake up at 7am, pray, and get ready for work. Work from 9:30am to 6pm with the rest of my evening completely free. It's not that watching TV is inherently bad. The problem was that it was taking time that I could have been investing in the kingdom and also reaping a reward.

---

50   Hebrews 12:6
51   Isaiah 40:31
110

Although we should not serve God solely because of a reward but out of love and devotion, there is a blessing in serving. Paul in Hebrews 6:10 says: "God is not unjust; he will not forget your work and the love you have shown him as you have helped his people and continue to help them."[52]

Identify Time Stealers

In Matthew 9:38, Jesus is calling us to pray for laborers, but as you pray for laborers, God is calling you to become a laborer as well.

One of the reasons people do not answer the call is because of a lack of balance. Everyone is busy. You may struggle with balance yourself. I have realized it is not that we fail to balance, but that we carry too much.

Trust me, I understand the number of things you are juggling. I am currently writing this book in my office at work in the Emergency Department where I work 40 hours a week, while working on a 3-year part-time master's program, trying to get my Christian apparel line off the ground, among other responsibilities. So, when the word *balance* is brought up, I know a thing or two about it.

End Your Struggle with Balance

You know what God told me when I asked Him for balance? He said, "Keep me in the center and I'll help you balance

---

everything." God was drawing my attention to Matthew 6:33: "But seek ye first the kingdom of God, and his righteousness; and all these things shall be added unto you."[53]

This is God's promise to you. If you are struggling with balance in your personal life, which has kept you away from using your gifts and talents in the expansion of God's kingdom, it's time to dig deep and find out why. You may even feel unqualified to carry out the work of the kingdom, but I want to tell you that the work on the cross qualifies you. If Christ has delivered you from the bondage of sin and the grave, you have a testimony to share.

Give God your YES!

Are you relying on your church and not contributing to its ability to function? Your church needs a greeter; someone to serve in the children's ministry; someone to lead outreaches, women's groups, and prayer meetings; yet you are sitting comfortably in the pews. And do not even say you pay your tithes and offerings because that 10% was already God's. That is not a contribution. You are only returning it to Him.[54]

God has posted a job and is awaiting your yes. Answer the call of God. Think about the many men and women who gave God their yes in the Bible:

---

53 King James Version (KJV)
54 Read The Blessed Life by Robert Morris for a better understanding of tithes, offerings, and extravagant giving.

- Moses gave God his yes and God used him to deliver the Israelites out of 400 years of Egyptian slavery to the wilderness where He met with them.

- Joshua gave God his yes and God used him to destroy the walls of Jericho and lead the Israelites into Canaan.

- Jeremiah gave God his yes and God used him as a mighty prophet to warn the Israelites of things to come and to repent.

- Mary gave God her yes and through her, our Savior was born.

Imagine the many things God will do through you with your YES. God does not call the qualified but qualifies the called. Jesus called Simon who denied Him three times, and Judas who sold Him for 30 pieces of silver. It is not your qualifications that God is looking for. All you need to do is answer the call to follow Him and He will make you a fisher of men.[55] As you follow Jesus, He will equip you with the necessary tools to become a laborer in His vineyard.

> "Just like we have our earthly work, we have a kingdom assignment to do. Each one of us collaborates with God. We need to be like day laborers who jump into the back of the truck for whatever work lies ahead. Instead, we go 'What's going to be my

---

55   Matthew 4:19

job? Does it fit in with my gift mix? Is that my personality profile? And how many days off am I going to get? I need to have balance.' We need to be a group of people that goes, 'Father, I want to be about your business today. I'm turning up and I am a day laborer for you.'"

—Christine Cain

So, let us PRAY *this*:

Heavenly Father, thank You for considering me qualified to be a laborer in Your vineyard. I am honored to share the gospel with everyone around me, but sometimes I am too busy, feel unqualified, or feel shy. Please help me to be bold in my faith and to share my testimony to encourage others to seek a relationship with You. Today, I give You my YES! In Jesus's Name. Amen.

Reflection

Listen to the song Yes Lord by Antioch Music - When You Call and use the following prompts to kick off your reflection on this chapter, which you can write in the blank pages provided.

1. Is there anything currently stealing your time away from God? How could this be fixed?

2. Do you feel unqualified to serve God?

3. How can you serve in your church?

PRAY FOR THE SPREAD OF THE GOSPEL

"Pray that the Lord's message will spread rapidly and be honored wherever it goes, just as when it came to you."
-2 Thessalonians 3:1 (NLT)

I don't know about you, but when I began to read the Bible and develop a personal relationship with Jesus, my life changed for the better. Wouldn't you want that for everyone in the world? At my local church, Calvary Christian Church in Lynnfield, Massachusetts, we are so committed to spreading the gospel around the world that we have an entire month dedicated to it. Every October, missionaries we support around the world visit to give a praise report on how our giving and prayers have helped spread the gospel.

One of the missionaries I am privileged to have been able to meet and shake hands with is Bob Hoskins. Seventy-nine years of full-time preaching ministry and he's still preaching.

Bob began preaching at age seven, two weeks after he received the baptism of the Holy Spirit.

In 1959, during the National Day of Prayer[56], there was a prophecy that *Book of Hope*, a children's bible written by Bob Hoskins, would be given to Russian children. At that time, Russia was an iron curtain, and the Bible had been forbidden for 70 years, so it seemed impossible. When Bob returned to his office, he received a message from Swedish businessmen, who were taking container loads of food to distribute, that the Russians gave them permission to give 50,000 Bibles to the children. Bob recounts his experience by saying this news gave him goosebumps. He could not believe it. Indeed, it was a God move.

A couple of months later, the minister of religion for the whole Soviet Union called Bob and his son and gave them a permit to distribute 140 million copies of *Book of Hope*. They wanted one for every child in every school in the Soviet Union. They believed it had answers for the children. As of October 2022, *Book of Hope* has been distributed to 1,800,000,000 and counting and should have crossed the 2 billion mark by February 2023.

Bob says, "The power of the gospel is in the gospel; the incorruptible word of God. It's not in the sower but in the seed. Not in the messenger but in the message."

Paul, a missionary of the gospel, says: "Finally, dear brothers and sisters, we ask you to pray for us. Pray that the Lord's

---

56   The first Thursday in May.

message will spread rapidly and be honored wherever it goes, just as when it came to you." (2 Thessalonians 3:1 [NLT])

The word "rapidly" connotes urgency. Paul is urging us to pray that the gospel of Christ will spread quickly at a fast rate. Why? Because the end is near.

Yes, for many years, people have waited for the end, and there have been many false predictions of the end, but this we know for sure: "But about that day or hour no one knows, not even the angels in heaven, nor the Son, but only the Father." (Matthew 24:36 [NIV])

However, Jesus says: "And this gospel of the kingdom shall be preached in all the world for a witness unto all nations; and then shall the end come." (Matthew 24:14 [KJV])

It is not our duty to worry about the end or make predictions of when it will be. "The Lord isn't really being slow about his promise, as some people think. No, he is being patient for your sake. He does not want anyone to be destroyed, but wants everyone to repent." (2 Peter 3:9 [NLT])

We are to channel our energy, time, and finances into getting lost souls into the kingdom before it's too late. Paul is asking that the gospel of Christ be spread far and wide and that wherever it is preached, it will be received. Paul said this knowing full well that people will still reject the gospel and he would have to follow Jesus' instructions: "If anyone will not welcome you or listen to your words, leave that home or town and shake the dust off your feet." (Matthew 10:14 [NIV])

A Word About Resistance in Others

Proclaiming the gospel is spiritual warfare. We should expect resistance when sharing the gospel. Even the disciples were met with resistance!

Our duty is to pray, remembering that "our struggle is not against flesh and blood, but against the rulers, against the authorities, against the powers of this dark world and against the spiritual forces of evil in the heavenly realms." (Ephesians 6:12 [NIV]) We should also pray for ideas on how to spread the gospel.

Jesus Is Calling You to Serve

Just as Jesus called the twelve, He is calling you today. Just as He equipped them, He is equipping you today. And like He sent them out, He wants to send you out and has given you "authority to drive out impure spirits and to heal every disease and sickness." (Matthew 10:1b [NIV]) Will you answer the call?

Does Your Life Bring God Fame?

It is my hope that as you read this, you decide to go on a mission trip, but while you're making plans, you can be a missionary right where you are. You do not have to travel out of the country to start sharing the gospel. You can start today at your workplace, at your school, on the bus—anywhere you go. You can start by asking the Holy Spirit to lead you to the people who need to hear your testimony the most.

Perhaps you are unable to physically go on a mission trip. In the words of my senior pastor, "If you cannot go, give, and if you cannot give, pray." However, I hope you get to experience the joy of going, giving *and* praying.

So, let us PRAY *this*:

Heavenly Father, thank You for calling us to the field to spread the gospel far and wide. Just like the many people in the Bible who said yes to your call, we say "Yes, Lord." We humble ourselves to be equipped to spread the light of God wherever we go. We pray against any resistance to the gospel. Let Your will be done and Your kingdom come on earth as it is in heaven. In Jesus's Name. Amen.

Reflection

Listen to the song "This Is the Kingdom by Elevation Worship and use the following prompts to kick off your reflection on this chapter, which you can write in the blank pages provided.

1. What are some hindrances to the spread of the gospel in your community?

2. In what ways can you share the gospel home and abroad?

PRAY FOR THOSE IN AUTHORITY

"First of all, then, I urge that petitions [specific requests], prayers, intercessions [prayers for others] and thanksgivings be offered on behalf of all people, for kings and all who are in [positions of] high authority, so that we may live a peaceful and quiet life in all godliness and dignity."
-I Timothy 2:1 (AMP)

The first ever election I was able to vote in was the election between Hillary Clinton and Donald Trump. I had never utilized such power before, and although I did not conduct proper research into their campaigns, I felt the obligation to vote, so that's what I did.

I remember that election period being very heightened, especially in church. The coronavirus and civil unrest during Donald Trump's presidency took things to another level where we could no longer ignore the facts in front of us. We needed a leader who would bring people together and not incite fear and hate.[57]

This book is not about politics, nor do I have the mental capacity to dissect politics, and I don't intend to do so. A wise man once said to "vote policies, not candidates because policies outlive candidates." Nonetheless, the decisions of politicians affect us all; therefore, we must pray for those in authority.

In 1 Timothy 2:1, Paul urges that prayers and thanksgiving be made for people in high authority so they may live a peaceful and quiet life in all godliness and dignity.

Some chapters ago, we learned to pray **for** those who hurt us, with an emphasis on parental figures. God has placed our parents in authority over us, as well as the government, which we are called to submit to. Romans 13:1-7 speaks about submission to governing authorities. Its countercultural tone makes it all the more striking.

Paul states that governments are ordained by God because He is a God of order and structure, and the alternative is chaos. In Genesis 1 & 2, it is evident that there was order in God's creation. God has ordained three institutions: family, church, and government. He placed the figures of authority in those institutions. It is in our best interest to recognize those in authority and pay them respect—even if we don't agree with them.

---

57   This is in no way intended to push any political belief.

When Paul writes this letter to the Romans, Nero was the emperor. Nero was known as one of the most wicked emperors ever to rule Rome and the one possibly responsible for Paul losing his head—yet Paul writes to be subject to governing authorities,[58] thus emphasizing God's command on the subject.

The Difference Between Obeying God and Obeying Man

Submission to authority does not necessarily mean obeying everything they tell you to do.

In Exodus 1, Pharaoh said to kill all the Hebrew baby boys, but the Hebrew midwives disobeyed him. Because of this, Moses is saved and later becomes the deliverer of the Israelites.

In Daniel 3, the Hebrew boys were told to bow down before the carved image of King Nebuchadnezzar. They refused because the second commandment in Exodus 20:5 states that we shall not bow down to or serve any graven image. They were thrown into a furnace of blazing fire, but no harm came to them, causing King Nebuchadnezzar to recognize the God of the Hebrew boys and make the boys prosperous.

In Daniel 6, Daniel prayed to God even after authorities issued a decree stating that no one should pray. Because of Daniel's disobedience, he was thrown into the lion's den

---

58   "Let every person be subject to the governing authorities. For there is no authority except from God [granted by His permission and sanction], and those which exist have been put in place by God." (Romans 13:1 [AMP])

but came out unharmed. This led to King Darius issuing a new decree that everyone should fear and revere the God of Daniel.

In Acts 5, Peter and John were arrested and put in a public jail for preaching the gospel. At night, an angel of the Lord opened the door of the prison and let them out with a command to "Go, stand in the temple courts...and tell the people all about this new life."[59] Although the religious leaders gave strict warnings to not preach in Jesus's Name, Peter and John continued to do so. When confronted by the religious leaders, their response was, "We must obey God rather than human beings!" (Acts 5:29 [NIV])

When the government gives you an order to disobey God, it is your responsibility to obey God first and always. When dealing with those in power you disagree with and when confronting sticky situations, go back to prayer. Use prayer as it was intended.

Prayer Is the Antidote to Dealing with Conflict

In Romans 13:1, Paul urges everyone to line up under and honor those above them in rank. No one is exempt from this rule. Same as you love your enemies and pray for them, you do not need to agree with your government officials to honor and respect them. Although our human nature is moved to throw curses at candidates we abhor who come into governing positions, James tells us that this is not right. He tells us

---

59   New International Version (NIV)

that blessing and cursing should not come pouring out of the same mouth.[60]

God works through wicked rulers. Looking to Jesus's answer to Pilate in John 19:10-11, "You would have no authority over me at all unless it had been given you from above,"[61] we need to submit to God's sovereignty. We need to decide if our lives are in the hands of human authority or if God is the highest authority in our lives, working through human authority to accomplish His divine purposes even when it is unfair, painful and undeserved.[62] Romans 8:28 gives us confidence that God works everything for our good.

We are called to respect, honor and PRAY for those in authority over us from presidents to supervisors at work. Don't talk disrespectfully about them. There's no perfect church, but we must honor the institution and respect the leaders; there's no perfect parent, but we must honor and respect our parents; likewise, there's no perfect government, but we must honor the institution and respect its leaders.

It is time we start trusting God's Word and doing more than voting. We need to pray and have faith that God is in control of our communities, schools, cities, states, and this nation.

---

60   James 3:10
61   English Standard Version (ESV)
62   Study Genesis chapters 39-41

So, let us PRAY *this*:

Heavenly Father, I come to you today to ask for forgiveness for any way I have rebelled against the authorities you have placed in my life. 1 Samuel 15:23 states that rebellion is as sinful as witchcraft, and stubbornness as bad as worshiping idols. I repent of my rebellion and stubbornness. Please give me the grace to honor and respect the authorities over my life. Help me not to utter curses against them but rather to speak life over them as it is not Your desire that anyone perishes but that they come to the knowledge of Christ Jesus. And in seasons when those authorities go against Your Word, may I have the courage like the Hebrew midwives, Daniel, and the three Hebrew boys to obey you first no matter the consequence. In Jesus's Name. AMEN.

Resource: Christians & Submission to Authority | Pastor Tim Schmidt

Reflection

Listen to the song "In Jesus' Name" by Darlene Zschech and use the following prompts to kick off your reflection on this chapter, which you can write in the blank pages provided.

1. Why is it difficult to obey God's Word over the government?

2. Have you ever been caught between obeying the government and obeying God? What did you do? What was the outcome?

3. What actions can you take to respect God-ordained authorities?

PRAY FOR EACH OTHER

"Confess your sins to each other and pray for each other so that you may be healed. The earnest prayer of a righteous person has great power and produces wonderful results."
—James 5:16 (NLT)

In Pastor Ron Carpenter's video series called *G-mail* (God mail), he talks about how heaven is like a courtroom. God is the mighty wise judge, and Jesus is the defense attorney for man. The testimony of the blood is evidence of you as a new creature to the great cloud of witnesses—saints of God gone on before us and the prosecutor also known as the accuser of the brethren, aka the devil. The major difference between the earthly and heavenly courtroom is that in the heavenly courtroom, instead of finding you guilty and locking you up for many years, after you've confessed, you are actually set free!

To confess means to admit wrongdoing. It is difficult to confess because after one has done so, their internal sin is now open for the judgmental eyes of the world, especially if you are in a position of high authority. However, Proverbs 28:13 says: "Whoever conceals their sins does not prosper, but the one who confesses and renounces them finds mercy."[63]

I always wondered why I should confess to someone else when I've already confessed my sins to God. The truth is that when you confess your sins, it breaks the stronghold of guilt and shame the devil has on you and, as James mentions, it produces healing. Healing here does not only attribute to physical healing but also emotional and spiritual healing.

Confessing is like therapy. You need to be willing to be transparent and vulnerable. You must go into the places and spaces that have been locked up for years and clean them out. It might be dusty and make you cough or sneeze. It may even move you to tears, but when you smell the clean fresh air around you that will result from this cleaning, you'll know it's all worth it. Over time, you will develop the habit of quick confession to avoid years of bondage.

I've had my own share of confessing, and it was never easy. I've had to put away my anger and pride to confess to friends, acquaintances, and family. In the cancel culture that we see ourselves in where we have little to no grace for people who make mistakes, forgetting that we ourselves are imperfect humans capable of hurting others, James is calling us to take a moment to confess and pray and be healed. It's all about extending grace and being vulnerable enough to say, "Hey,

---

63   New King James Version (NKJV)

this is where I fell short or what I'm struggling with. Can you pray with me so I can be healed?" Healing is the fruit of confessions and prayer.

Relationships Take Work

I am reminded of Paul's instruction for us to "work at living in peace with everyone." (Hebrews 12:14a [NLT]) The key word is "work." Things do not just change if you don't make an effort to participate in the process.

I attended Joyce Myers's conference once where she shared about the physical and emotional abuse she endured at the hands of her father and mother growing up. I was bittered by her story. Then she shared how God told her that she was to move her father close to her house and take care of him, and she did, which led to his repentance and salvation.

Prior to hearing from God, Joyce visited her father in the hospital and he said, "Joyce, I am sorry you feel I hurt you. But I still don't understand what was so bad about what I did." After Joyce obeyed God's lead, her father called her and said, "I am sorry for what I did to you. I have wanted to say this to you for a long time, but I didn't have the guts." Indeed, it is God's love that compels us to repentance. God shows His love through you and me.

God Gives the Strength to Confess

The God I know is a God of restitution. He will direct you on the next steps, and no matter how difficult, take them.

135

You can also confess to a mentor or an elder in the church who will pray for you and turn your focus back to listening to God as to what to do next.

The second part of James 5:16 says that *"the earnest prayer of a righteous person has great power and produces wonderful results."* Joyce's father's salvation did not come immediately, but the continuous prayer and love from Joyce had great power to move her father to repentance.

Patience and Prayer

In our society today, we want instant results. Our patience wears thin, and I must confess patience is my least prominent virtue. We must persevere during the process of confessing, praying, and healing as God is faithful to restore us. James 5:16 says, "The heartfelt and **persistent** prayer of a righteous man…"[64] While I do believe in instantaneous miracles, there is some healing that will require persistent prayers. Do not grow weary in praying continuously for healing.

You Are Not God, So Don't Judge Others

A word of advice: when people who identify as Christians come to you to confess, do not judge them.[65] You are not God. "You may think you can condemn such people, but you are just as bad, and you have no excuse! When you say they are wicked and should be punished, you are condemning

---

64   Amplified Bible (AMP)
65   Mark 16:15

yourself, for you who judge others do these very same things." (Romans 2:1 [NLT])

There is an old adage that says, "When you point a finger at someone, four fingers are pointing back at you." When a brother or sister in Christ falls into sin, it should be a time of reflection for us to look inward.

Spiritual Things Are Slippery

One of my favorite sayings is found in 1 Corinthians 10:12: "So if you think you are standing firm, be careful that you don't fall!"

This is a warning to those who are convinced of their own righteousness. Even the Bible says a righteous man falleth seven times; not an unrighteous man.[66] Being a Christian does not mean perfection, free of sin. It means we don't have to pay the penalty as Jesus already did, and most importantly, it means we have the Holy Spirit to help us in this journey on earth.

As we pray for each other, we are engaging in what the Bible calls Prayer of Agreement. In Matthew 18:19, Jesus says: "Again I say to you, that if two believers on earth agree [that is, are of one mind, in harmony] about anything that they ask [within the will of God], it will be done for them by My Father in heaven."[67]

---

66   Job 5:19
67   Amplified Bible (AMP)

I always wondered why Jesus did not just say, "If any of you makes up his mind and asks within the will of God, it will be done." But He said, "two believers." There must be power in two believers, let alone more than two.

Today, confess to someone and welcome their prayer for healing. If you are the confidant, resist the urge to be judgmental. Listen and genuinely pray for the confessor. Furthermore, work to restore that person gently,[68] and if you do not have the capacity to do so, ask the confessor's permission to bring someone in who can.

So, let us PRAY *this*:

Heavenly Father, I understand that confessing leads to healing. I need healing in (mention the areas). Please give me the confidence to confess and receive prayers so I may be healed. If I am the confidant, help me to put away my judgmental attitude. Help me to listen, pray, and point the confessor back to You. In Jesus's Name. Amen.

---

68   1 John 5:16

Reflection

Listen to the song "The Cross Is My Confession" by Kari Jobe and use the following prompts to kick off your reflection on this chapter, which you can write in the blank pages provided.

1. Have you ever confessed to someone? What did it feel like? Would you do it again?

2. How can you be a safe space for someone to confess?

PRAY WITHOUT CEASING

"Be unceasing and persistent in prayer."
-1 Thessalonians 5:17 (AMP)

This is one of the first scriptures I memorized. So easy to memorize, yet not as easy to put into practice. This whole book is about prayer—what to pray and how to pray. However, prayer is not just something you do once. Prayer requires consistency. Just like you can't go to the gym once and expect to have a perfectly toned body that day. The same goes for prayer. In prayer, we build our spiritual muscles. Muscles of self-control, discipline, love, humility, kindness, gentleness, faithfulness, forgiveness, perseverance, and joy.[69]

It always astonishes me when I hear testimonies of how people prayed for a child, waiting many years, and God answered

---

69   Galatians 5:22-23

their prayer. Hannah is an example of this in the Bible. She was provoked and mocked by her sister wife Peninnah but loved immensely by her husband Elkanah who would give her a double portion of the sacrificial meat.[70] Waiting to receive something you have been praying for is painful. It can cause what Hannah mentioned as "a despairing spirit." To despair means to show the loss of all hope, yet she prayed when all hope was lost.

In today's world, we are lucky to have advanced technology that improves the quality of our lives. People living in more advanced countries like the U.S. take things for granted, like the water flowing from their tap and access to emergency care, while people a flight away cannot enjoy these privileges. We've been termed "the Microwave Generation," which is important to pay attention to. We want instant gratification, but unfortunately, prayer doesn't always work this way.

God is not a genie in a bottle—and thank God He's not because we know what happens when man's selfish desires are granted.

In Luke 18:1-8, Jesus was telling His disciples a parable to make a point: we ought always to pray and not give up and lose heart. Jesus told His disciples the story of a judge who had no fear of God nor respect for man, and certainly not for a certain widow who had kept coming to him for justice and legal protection from her adversary.

---

70   1 Samuel

One day, this judge decided to grant this widow her demands because of her persistence:

> "Then the Lord said, 'Listen to what the unjust judge says! And will not [our just] God defend *and* avenge His elect [His chosen ones] who cry out to Him day and night? Will He delay [in providing justice] on their behalf? I tell you that He will defend *and* avenge them quickly. However, when the Son of Man comes, will He find [this kind of persistent] faith (prayer) on the earth?"[71]

What is it that you stopped praying about? Who is that person you stopped praying for? Reflect in the notes section provided and continue to pray. Pray without ceasing and God, the just judge, will answer you.

So, let us PRAY *this*:

Heavenly Father, sometimes it's hard to persist in prayer. Help me to pray consistently even in despair because prayer builds my character. In Jesus's Name. Amen.

Reflection

Listen to the song "Pray Without Ceasing" by Edwin Hawkins and use the following prompts to kick off your reflection on this chapter, which you can write in the blank pages provided.

1. Who or what did you stop praying for and why?

2. How can you increase your faith to consistently pray?

AUTHOR BIO

Emmanuella Ofurie holds a BS in public health and is en route to getting her master's in public health nutrition. She serves on the Worship Team at her local church, Calvary Christian Church in Lynnfield, Massachusetts. She also accepts invitations to minister at other churches and volunteers to sing for Christian events.

PRAY this is Nuella's first book, but she has been writing blog posts and creating YouTube videos for some years. You can check them out on her website: www.nuellasnuggets.com

Some of her hobbies include dancing, cooking, writing, singing, weightlifting, and spending time alone with God. She hopes to continue to be used by God to produce Christian lifestyle content for ladies to remind them that they are gold.

Thank You for Reading My Book!

I really appreciate all of your feedback and
I love hearing what you have to say.

Please take two minutes now to leave a helpful review on
Amazon letting me know what you thought of the book:
Thanks so much!
—Emmanuella Ofurie

selfpublishing.com

NOW IT'S YOUR TURN

Discover the EXACT 3-step blueprint you need to become a bestselling author in as little as 3 months.

Self-Publishing School helped me, and now I want them to help you with this FREE resource to begin outlining your book!

Even if you're busy, bad at writing, or don't know where to start, you CAN write a bestseller and build your best life. With tools and experience across a variety of niches and professions, Self-Publishing School is the only resource you need to take your book to the finish line!

DON'T WAIT

Say "YES" to becoming a bestseller:

https://selfpublishing.com/friend/

Follow the steps on the page to get a FREE resource to get started on your book and unlock a discount to get started with SelfPublishing.com

Made in the USA
Middletown, DE
28 August 2023